SAVOR THE FLAVORS

Volume 2

A Beginner's Guide to Cigars

Chef CT

Dedication

To all the cigars enthusiasts who truly savor the flavors, cheers!

Acknowledgment

Chef CT thanks God, first and foremost. For the ability to get this reading out to those who don't understand or know where, or how to get started on their cigar journey. Thanks to those of you who took the time to read this manuscript to help you venture into the world of Cigars, while Savoring the Flavors of Cigars.

About the Author

Chef CT is a culinary-trained chef with a passion for helping people understand their flavor profiles. He is a co-owner of The Mason Cigar Manor, a cigar shop and lounge in Mason, OH. Chef offers cigar and whiskey pairings, as well as cigar and wine, and cigar and coffee pairings to enhance people's experiences.

Hello friends! Chef CT here. Welcome to Savor The Flavors Volume 2. In Volume 1, we learned a few basics about some of the flavor notes in Whisk(e)y. With this, second volume of our series, Savor the Flavors, Volume 2: A Beginner's Guide to Cigars, we'll talk about some of the flavor notes, you can expect to experience, while you "Savor the Flavors" while enjoying premium cigars. As you read this volume, I'm going to walk you through a cigar-smoking experience, as we discuss flavor notes, a brief overview of how premium cigars are made, and other tips. My hope is that Savor the Flavors Volume 2: A Beginner's Guide to Cigars will help you gain a basic understanding of cigars and the cigar culture.

As I stated in volume 1, I am not a professional cigar blender or roller; however, I am a culinary-trained chef with a passion for premium cigars. I have a very sensitive palate. I like experiencing the different flavor profiles of premium cigars, as well as the relaxation I get while enjoying a premium cigar, and sharing my thoughts with others.

First things, first, don't get too overwhelmed or frustrated as you venture into your cigar smoking journey, as there are a plethora of cigars to try. The cigar culture is rapidly growing worldwide at the time of this writing. At one time, the Tampa Bay, Florida area (Ybor City) was considered the premium cigar capital of the United States. Today, Miami, Florida, shares the title with Ybor City, Florida, as the premier premium cigar area in the United States. My apologies, you didn't purchase the book to get a cigar history lesson, although there may be a few historical points as we go on. Let's get you started, enjoying your cigar smoking experience.

There are different types of cigars. For Savor the Flavors, volume 2, we're going to focus on premium cigars. Premium cigars are all natural. There are no preservatives or chemicals introduced to the tobacco plants at any time, from the time the cigar seed is planted, to the time the cigar is rolled, until the time you begin to smoke it. We won't dive into every step of the cigar-making process, as there are so many steps taken to make a premium cigar. We will, however, share a brief overview to help you understand what goes into making a finely crafted, premium cigar. Let me say upfront, we do NOT inhale cigar smoke.

Cigar smoke has a high alkaline content. The lungs in the human body don't handle the high level of alkalinity from cigars as they can cigarette smoke (which is more acidic). Thus, people inhale cigarette smoke almost always. Cigar smoking is about savoring the flavor profile of the cigar. There are so many ways to create different flavor profiles in a cigar. The manufacturers of premium cigars are masterminds at understanding the characteristics of the soil, climate, surrounding nature, etc... Different regions, of different countries (such as the Dominican Republic, Cuba, Nicaragua, Ecuador, Honduras, etc...) have very rich soils that can (and does) produce great tobacco for cigars. In addition, there are so many other factors that open up and bring out the flavors within a cigar leaf, from a particular cigar tobacco farm (or region).

For example, as I stated in Savor the Flavors, Volume 1, A Beginners Guide to Whiskey, if there is an Orange Grove, or herb farm, within 20 miles of a tobacco farm, nature has a way of imparting some of those flavors into the stalk of the cigar tobacco, via rain, wind, animal droppings, etc... Once the tobacco seedling has grown enough to be planted in the field, it then grows to a matured tobacco plant. This process involves farmers meticulously tending to the plants daily to ensure the leaves needed for cigars are of the highest quality. When the cigar is ready for harvesting, the workers pick the leaves from the plant (stalk), then hang them for a while (a certain amount of time). As the leaves hang in a barn, they release chlorophyll, which turns the color of the leaves from green to brown (as well as a few other toxins). Once they reach a desired color, the tobacco leaves are piled up into groupings to ferment. As they ferment, they release ammonia and the remaining chlorophyll. Once the manufacturer is pleased with the fermentation process, the aging process can begin. As the tobacco ages, some of those flavor notes (as mentioned earlier) will concentrate and may be noticeable while smoking that particular cigar. The aging stage is where a lot of the magic happens for the cigar tobacco leaves. Let's talk briefly about the aging stage of cigar making.

Different manufacturers age their tobacco leaves to achieve different strengths and maturity levels to achieve different flavor profiles. There are different stages to consider while maturing cigar tobacco. Let's use a banana to give an example of how aging and ripening go hand in hand. I have a green banana. If I were to peel and eat the green banana, it would be somewhat bitter, with a hint of sweetness. However, if I set the green banana on a table or countertop, as the days go by, the banana ripens. Its color will literally change from green to yellow, to dark yellow, to brown, to black. With each passing day, the banana peel gets darker, due to the sugars concentrating, thus ripening.

Cigar tobacco does somewhat the same thing; as it ages, it creates different flavor profiles. As cigar leaves age, they will change colors (creating different flavor profiles during each stage of color changing), hence, the different colors of cigar leaves (as you will see when searching for a cigar to smoke). As the leaves age, they ripen. That is a whole book on its own, so we won't get too deep into that. This is merely a brief overview of what happens to the tobacco leaves as they age. Once the leaves are aged, per the master blender, the cigar leaves are rolled into finely crafted forms, which we call cigars. After being rolled, the cigars are placed in a giant humidor, of sorts, to marry.

Marrying is the stage of the cigar-making process where the oils from the different leaves within the newly formed cigar join together to form the flavor profiles we've grown to love and enjoy. As you're just starting on your cigar smoking journey, your taste buds will determine what flavor profile YOU enjoy. I know many people who only smoke cigars wrapped in a lighter shade. Those are often referred to as Claro (light tan colored) or Connecticut Shade. The perception is, the lighter the wrapper, the less potent the cigar will be. Personally, I will smoke a cigar, no matter the wrapper color. I will research the particular cigar to determine its blend and strength. As I am an avid smoker, I prefer a Maduro or Oscuro wrapper. Maduro basically translates to "ripe," while Oscuro translates to "dark or black."

The wrapper gives us between 85%-90% of the flavor of the cigar. The perception is, the darker the wrapper, the stronger the cigar. To a certain extent, that can be true. Cigar blenders are very good at creating milder cigars, using a Maduro, Habano, Cameroon, or even Oscuro wrapper. Generally, if I'm introducing someone new to a cigar, I'll steer them to a lighter Connecticut shade cigar (such as a NUB Connecticut, or Perdomo 10th Anniversary Champagne). After they've been smoking for a while, I'll step them up to a Connecticut Broadleaf (shade-grown), which can be a little stronger in body, but a lot more flavorful. If you enjoy spicy flavors (such as black pepper and herbs), please don't let a darker wrapper deter you from enjoying your cigar smoking experience. If you go to a brick-and-mortar (local cigar shop or lounge), the tobacconist on hand will help you pick out a great cigar for you to enjoy, even as a novice smoker. FYI, tobacconists are there to help you, so please ask questions.

As an example, I always ask a beginner cigar smoker what their preferred beverage is. I can then steer them to a premium cigar to complement their beverage, thus heightening their cigar-smoking experience. Tobacconists are knowledgeable about the cigars they carry in their shops or lounges. Tobacconists love to help answer your questions, so please don't hesitate to ask if you're unsure. We want your cigar-smoking experience to be the best experience, every time.

We finally have our cigar in hand and ready to light up. Personally, I usually SLIGHTLY squeeze the foot of the cigar (the end that will be burning) prior to lighting, to ensure the cigar has been humidified at a respectable level (cigars love to be humidified between 68-72 degrees, relative humidity, and 70 degrees relative temperature). If the foot cracks, it could be a sign; the wrapper could unravel during your smoking experience. Next, I cut the head (the end of the cigar that you will draw from). I use a V-cut, straight cut, or punch. Your method of cutting is entirely up to you. You will know which type of cut you prefer over time, as there are multitudes of ways to cut your cigar. If you're unsure of which cut to select, please ask your tobacconist or friends what they suggest. Now that we've cut our cigar, let's take a cold draw. A cold draw is the step of drawing from the cigar before it's lit. A cold draw will hopefully reveal some subtle flavor notes you'll experience once you light up.

We're ready, friends, so let's light up (I'm excited for you)! There are quite a few ways to light a cigar. We won't get too deep into this, as during your cigar smoking journey, YOU will ultimately decide which method YOU prefer. There are many ways to light a cigar, such as longer wooden matches, single, double, triple, or even quad flamed torches (lighters), a strip of cedar, etc. I'll use a quad flamed torch for this reading. I start by holding the flame about 2 inches away from the foot of the cigar. Slowly toast the foot of the cigar, while turning the cigar either clockwise or counterclockwise, until the foot is completely lit. You will recognize this by the foot glowing orange and smoke, emanating from the cigar (signifying it's burning).

Just a side note, before we take our first draw, it may be helpful to know that some people smoke fast, and some smoke slow. I am a fast smoker. I will usually take a draw, between 60-90 seconds apart. I have some friends who will draw every two to three minutes (or more). When I first began on my cigar journey, the place I purchased my cigars from told me to draw every three to four minutes. I found myself having to relight my cigars constantly. Now, take a draw. Remember, DON'T INHALE! Savor the flavors, then, blow the smoke out.

Ask yourself if you recognize or taste any of the flavors you experienced with the cold draw. If so, what flavors do you taste? Some of the more prominent flavors that are noticeable in premium cigars across the board are leather, earthiness, hay, heavy cream, dark cacao, herbs (rosemary, thyme, white pepper, black pepper, red pepper, etc), dark cacao (dark, bitter, 70+% pure chocolate) and coffee bean. Most of the cigars you smoke will have either, more, or less, of the above mentioned, and may have some other notes that you notice, such as a floral note, sweetness, molasses, etc... Master blenders are great at creating blends of cigars that have distinct flavor profiles, separating one from another.

As we begin smoking our cigars, let us understand that cigars are classified in thirds (first-third, second-third, and final-third). Generally, within the first-third, you will pick up the most noticeable flavor note(s). In my experience, the first-third, will reveal a couple of prominent flavor notes, as well as some that are barely there. The ones that are barely there, you might pick them up, or you may even think your mind is playing tricks on your taste buds. Remember, we

9

are savoring the flavors. Can you identify any specific flavor notes?

Do you taste leather? Do you taste the spice of black pepper? How about the herbiness of rosemary or thyme? Do you pick up any roasted coffee bean notes? Is there any hint of dark chocolate? One of the great things about the cigar smoking experience is the relaxation. For a brief period of time, you are free from your stresses. As we unwind from a long day, we are free to savor the flavors of our cigar. At this time, we should be entering the second-third of our cigar. As you draw and exhale, your ash may get long or flake off. Ash your cigar periodically. When we ash our cigars, we don't want to beat the cigar on our ashtray. We want to simply roll the ash into the ashtray. Beating the cigar to ash it may damage the lit tobacco, causing an uneven burn. During the second-third, one or more flavor notes, which we identified at lighting, will either become more prominent or fade away. I usually notice one or two flavor notes get more prominent, while others either fade away completely or fall almost dim. Let me ask you, which flavor note have you noticed coming on stronger? Is that flavor note dominating? Do you taste that note with each draw? Are other flavor notes marrying well, in harmony, to allow you to enjoy your smoking experience? Let's take our time and truly explore and experience savoring the flavors of these finely crafted cigars.

As we enter the final third, you will definitely notice one or more flavor notes, constantly, from here until the end. The final-third, is where the cigar will, more than likely, get stronger to you. Possibly, this could be due to the fire being closer to your draw point (your mouth), causing the oils of the cigar leaves to be heated up closer to the draw point. If this is true, you could feel a little lightheaded. If you do happen to feel a little lightheaded, drink some water to rehydrate yourself. Your ash should be close to the band at this point. Feel free to take the band off and continue to enjoy your finely crafted cigar. I know quite a few people who are finished with their cigar once they reach the band. Personally, I smoke my cigars down to the nub. I'm not going to extinguish a fine cigar before it's time.

One last piece of advice: after you've finished smoking your cigar, don't tamp it out like you would with a cigarette. Just leave it alone. The cigar will go out on its own within five minutes. By tamping the cigar out, a toxic gas will be released from the cigar. If you inhale those toxins, you run the risk of symptoms, such as nausea or dizziness, so simply let the cigar go out on its own.

I am anxious for you to enjoy your journey into the world of cigars. As you learn to savor the flavors of cigars, don't be afraid to pick the brains of your tobacconist, friend, or even the person you just sat down next to in the cigar lounge. One thing about the cigar community, no matter where you're from, what you do for a living, your race, creed, or cultural background, sharing a cigar with someone—whether you know them well or just met—sitting together and smoking cigars brings us ALL closer. I met my group of friends a few short years ago. What started out as a group of five guys, smoking a cigar or two, every Thursday eve, has turned into a group of 15 (or more), smoking and enjoying, quality, premium cigars, while sipping on good, premium Whisk(e)y, Scotch, and/or wine, while forgetting our troubles, and stresses, for a few hours.

We've earned each other's trust, as far as to be able to help each other find solutions to our personal problems, work problems, and even world problems. The bond formed through the cigar culture is truly remarkable. As you journey into Savoring the Flavors of Premium Cigars, don't be afraid to meet someone you don't know. Please don't be afraid to try a different cigar. Each time you visit your local brick-and-mortar or lounge (whether in your hometown or outside of your hometown), please open up your mind and heart to try a new cigar. There are so many options out there, you're bound to find one, two, three, or more that appeal to YOUR taste buds. There are so many manufacturers, with so many good blends of cigars. Don't deny yourself the opportunity to experience greatness from a manufacturer you may grow to love. I try to smoke a new cigar, or two, every week. I love having the option of leaving my options open. I will say, I do have a few favorites that I call go-to's. I keep those certain cigars in my home humidors, as well as my travel humidors. How was your cigar? I hope you enjoyed Savoring the Flavors of your Cigar, as we journeyed through it together. As a final thought and wish, I want to bid you a hearty "Bon Appétit" and "Cheers," my friend! Please join us for Savor the Flavors Volume 3: A Beginner's Guide to Wine Tasting. Until next time, cigar family, I hold my cigar up to you and bid you CHEERS!

CHEF

The End

www.ingramcontent.com/pod-product-compliance
Lightning Source LLC
Chambersburg PA
CBHW051254120626
46547CB00014B/1941